"Toddy Hoare's imaginative re-telling of the apostle Peter's story gives us an accessible and insightful account of the life and work of the early church. What shines through Hoare's approach to Saint Peter's ministry is just how precarious it was . . . not just living hand-to-mouth but also figuring out where the next call to be comes from and where it leads next. This is an intriguing and unusual book which will resonate with all who engage with it."

—MARTYN PERCY, Provost Theologian, Ming Hua College, Hong Kong

"This is a story which holds your attention from the very beginning, with 'Uncle Peter' being portrayed as a very human fisherman who grows to become the leader of the early church through his testing, with his failures being overcome by his perseverance and openness to Christ. It would make an ideal book to give to someone exploring the faith for the first time, with its vivid and direct style. I was enthralled by the story."

—PETER SEDGWICK, Former Principal, St. Michael's College Llandaff, Wales

"Drawing on the tradition that Mark's Gospel is based on the recollections of Peter, Toddy Hoare re-tells it as *Uncle Peter's Story*. This means that readers' minds are focused on the human response to the divine activity taking place in Jesus and experienced by Peter and Mark. This imaginative approach to the Bible may appeal not only to those unfamiliar with the Gospels, but also to those to whom they have become all too familiar."

—MORNA HOOKER, Lady Margaret's Professor Emerita, University of Cambridge

"In *Uncle Peter's Story*, [Toddy Hoare] brings the interaction between St. Peter and Jesus to life as if he was living amongst the apostles in ancient bible lands. It is all about Christ amongst the day to day lives of fishermen and artisans of the time and what must have been their amazed reaction to Jesus as he healed the sick, 'his power and popularity rather disrupted life and interrupted mealtimes!' Perhaps if more of us had read Bible texts so related to actual life amongst family and friends, we would have more belief and faith. I salute Toddy's work in bringing St. Mark's Gospel to life and hopefully more awareness amongst the family of the Church of England."

—GEORGE HERBERT, Eighth Earl of Carnarvon, England

Uncle Peter's Story

Uncle Peter's Story

Tracing St. Peter's Path to Spiritual Maturity

TODDY HOARE

Foreword by Andrew Briggs
Afterword by Martyn Percy

RESOURCE *Publications* · Eugene, Oregon

UNCLE PETER'S STORY
Tracing St. Peter's Path to Spiritual Maturity

Copyright © 2025 Toddy Hoare. All rights reserved. Except for brief quotations in critical publications or reviews, no part of this book may be reproduced in any manner without prior written permission from the publisher. Write: Permissions, Wipf and Stock Publishers, 199 W. 8th Ave., Suite 3, Eugene, OR 97401.

Resource Publications
An Imprint of Wipf and Stock Publishers
199 W. 8th Ave., Suite 3
Eugene, OR 97401

www.wipfandstock.com

PAPERBACK ISBN: 979-8-3852-5409-5
HARDCOVER ISBN: 979-8-3852-5410-1
EBOOK ISBN: 979-8-3852-5411-8

09/10/25

Dedicated to my Grandchildren and Great grandson as I write, along with any who would start exploring the scriptures to boost their belief and find a foundation for their faith.

Contents

Foreword by Andrew Briggs | ix

Acknowledgments | xiii

Introduction: Tracing St. Peter's Spiritual Formation in the New Testament | xv

Part 1. What Uncle Peter Did, as per St. Mark's Gospel | 1

Part 2. Peter as John heard through the eyes and ears of St. John's Gospel | 21

Part 3. St. Matthew on Peter | 25

Part 4. Uncle Peter's activities as recorded by Luke in The Acts of the Apostles | 27

Postscript: Thoughts Round Peter | 39

Index: The Old Testament references in Mark's gospel | 47

The Fishermen's Boat | 51

Afterword by Martyn Percy | 53

Foreword

THERE ARE MANY WAYS to bear witness to reality. I have written about this with Michael Reiss in our book *Human Flourishing*. It is what science seeks to do in systematically establishing a reliable body of knowledge, through methods that have been refined over many years. It is what a witness in a court of law promises to do, when they repeat the words, "I swear by Almighty God that the evidence which I shall give shall be the truth, the whole truth, and nothing but the truth." The secular alternative "I do solemnly, sincerely and truly declare and affirm that the evidence which I shall give shall be the truth, the whole truth, and nothing but the truth." is also acceptable. But how feasible is it to do that? If the witness says, "I saw the witness enter the building looking cheerful at 8 o'clock," a pedant might ask: with what precision did you determine the time, and what details might you have omitted in asserting that this is the whole truth, and anyway how do you establish the truth of someone looking cheerful? A scrupulous witness might add to their oath, "insofar as it is relevant to the case in hand, and insofar as it is sufficiently accurate and reliable to inform and not mislead the court for the purposes of the decision which the jury is required to reach." This would be a considerable qualification, and it might not be helpful to the jury.

A historian is faced with comparable challenges. They might seek to represent exactly what would be recorded on a video of a historical event. But which way to point the camera, and what zoom setting to use, and whose voice to record on the soundtrack, and how to edit it in post-production? The German historian Leopold von Ranke asked whether it was possible to write a history

FOREWORD

of what actually happened (*wie es eigentlich gewesen*). In German there are two words which convey different aspects of history: *Geshicte* = what happened and *Historie* = its interpretation. But the distinction implied by the arithmetic signs does not hold up. There is no such thing as an uninterpreted account of what happened. All accounts, whether of a world war or a natural disaster or a conversation with a friend, are interpreted through the mind and the perspective of the narrator.

That is as true of the gospels as it is of any other documentary evidence, and it is as true of Mark's gospel as it is of the other gospels. Just as the witness in a court of law can be faithful to their oath without succumbing to the niceties of the pedant, so too the gospel writer can give a faithful account of the life of Jesus Christ without having to include everything that he said and did, or even to report it in the same words as the other witnesses.

There is a further way to bear witness to the truth, that would not be allowed in a court of law, and a fortiori would be denied to our hidebound pedant. That is to use imagination. In just such a way J. R. R. Tolkien bore witness to deep insights about the way the world is through his narrative in a new fantasy world in *The Lord of the Rings*. Tolkien was adamant that this was not allegory; it was an imaginative creation. His fellow Inkling C. S. Lewis was more explicit in his articulation of his Christian faith, and more wide-ranging, from his seven Narnia stories for children (and also grown-ups) to his science fiction trilogy and non-fiction for grown-ups only. Tolkien, Lewis, and the other Inklings used their imagination to convey profound truth about the way the world is and the place of the Christian tradition within it.

Toddy Hoare has used his imagination to bring to life the Gospel of Mark. He achieves this by retelling the narrative as though it were the story of Peter, previously known as Simon, who was the first disciple to be called by Jesus together with his brother Andrew. After the account of Jesus' baptism, his period in the desert, and the beheading of John the Baptist, Peter would have observed at first hand almost everything recounted in Mark's Gospel, or at least learned about it immediately afterwards from someone

FOREWORD

else who had been there. The connection between Peter and Mark is variously alluded to in the New Testament, notably in the Acts of the Apostles and in the first letter attributed to Peter, and Toddy Hoare takes the warranted imaginative step of designating Mark as Peter's nephew. As Toddy somewhat colorfully described it to me in an email, "Mark is a bit like the younger brother of a girl you are chatting up suddenly popping up as he follows at a distance to see what happens. Jesus would certainly arouse a youngster's interest!" Seen in that light, Toddy Hoare has written a gripping retelling of Uncle Peter's story through the voice of his nephew Mark.

One of the first books I ever read at one sitting as a child was *The Lion, the Witch, and the Wardrobe*. I probably missed the subtlety of the dedication.

> My Dear Lucy,
> I wrote this story for you, but when I began it I had not realized that girls grow quicker than books. As a result you are already too old for fairy tales, and by the time it is printed and bound you will be older still. But some day you will be old enough to start reading fairy tales again. You can then take it down from some upper shelf, dust it, and tell me what you think of it. I shall probably be too deaf to hear, and too old to understand a word you say, but I shall still be your affectionate Godfather,
> C.S. Lewis

Many years later I was asked to speak at a school where the pupils were of roughly the same age as I had been when I first read the book. To get myself into an appropriate frame of mind therefore took it down from some upper shelf, dusted it, and re-read it. I found myself almost moved to tears as I now found in it much that had escaped me as a small child.

In just such a way, Toddy Hoare writes,

> Dedicated to my Grandchildren and Great grandson as I write, along with any who would start exploring the scriptures to boost their belief and find a foundation for their faith.

Foreword

As I read *Uncle Peter's Story*, I found myself no less engrossed than when I read *The Lion, the Witch, and the Wardrobe* the second time. I trust that grown-ups will enjoy Toddy Hoare's retelling of Uncle Peter's story just as much—albeit in different ways—as their children and grandchildren and beyond.

ANDREW BRIGGS, Professor of Nanomaterials, University of Oxford; author of *The Penultimate Curiosity, It Keeps Me Seeking*, and *Human Flourishing*.

Acknowledgments

AFTER A STRUGGLE PETER found spiritual maturity and that inner peace that passes all understanding and led the way forward from Pentecost. It was meaningful to be ordained on St. Peter's day proper in York Minster by Stuart Blanch and be presented by the then Archdeacon of York, Leslie Stanbridge, as Toddy after he had read out my four Christian names which caused a ripple of laughter throughout the Minster. (Leslie means Holly Garden but Leslie was only prickly if you did not strive for the best!) After years of training, study, and continued reading there are too many erudite teachers, lecturers and writers to mention not forgetting those still offering a wide range of commentaries. There is the old joke that you can tell where a priest's theology stops by looking on his bookshelf to see what he might have read recently. However I would single out Anthony Hanson, one of the terrible twins either end of the M62, whom I inherited as my honorary curate when I became a parish priest. He set out to improve and encourage my theology and I am ever grateful to him. The headstone for him, amongst many that I have cut over the years, stands in Felixkirk churchyard.

It was Anthony who set up the MA course at Hull University—A Theological Understanding of Industrial Society—and I was lucky enough to do it when Peter Sedgwick was running it and for whom, when he was Principal of St. Michael's Theological College at Llandaff, I staged a 3 year rolling exhibition of sculpture prompted by my studies of scripture. He also wrote the Foreword for my book of verse and sculpture—The Christ Cycle.

I would like to thank Andrew Briggs for his Foreword and those who will be asked in time to endorse this book as such

Acknowledgments

recognition is encouraging and also humbling because such support is needed on a venture and an idea that produces a book. Also to Martyn Percy as a friend, like Andrew, but a theologian who appreciated my daring to present a man's road to Spiritual maturity.

I cannot miss out mentioning my wife, Liz, with whom I share our respective fields of ministry that had first fruits in a combined Grove booklet: Sculpture, Prayer and Scripture.

Furthermore her time as director of the MTh at Oxford and as tutor in spiritual formation at Wycliffe gave me the space to develop expressing scripture in sculpture and verse and ensuring that my Bible exploration does not come to a halt. Together we have different ways of encouraging spiritual growth and understanding in the individual.

TODDY HOARE, Danby Wiske. June 2025.

Introduction

Tracing St. Peter's Spiritual Formation in the New Testament

THIS IS ST. PETER's road to spiritual maturity and the premier witness to the resurrection. As a starter I urge older people seeking Baptism or a way to start Lent to read St. Mark's Gospel straight through in one sitting like a short story—probably some 45 minutes. Not a bad way to be still! In turn this little volume aims to be a starter for younger people with a good reading age while a hors d'oeuvre for the busy older person. Also it allows for many these days used to smaller soundbites to orientate themselves before tackling a more in depth commentary. It is there to help people into exploring the Bible in greater detail starting with St. Mark's Gospel. By that stage a Bible of the reader's choice, since there are many translations and revised copies, may have footnotes, cross references, commentaries besides a wide range of background information that have been specifically written on each book, history, origin and aspect of the Bible.

It is generally considered that Mark was the nephew, rather than son, of Simon Peter, also called Simeon and the Rock (Petra or Cephas) by Jesus. As a boy of 8 or 9 I was much influenced by the story of St Mark on the back page of the Eagle—a weekly colorful comic launched in 1950 by the Revd. Marcus Morris. It was realistically illustrated and the narrative was written by the Revd. Chad

Introduction

Varar (1911–2007) who also founded The Samaritans Help Line in 1953. Needless to say such a background made my own studies at Wycliffe Theological College, Oxford, where Marcus Morris had been, a lot easier because the back story had been opened out.

I have kept the text simple and free of notes, writing from the Gospel as it struck me. I have not been dependent on commentaries though I have consulted many over the years in training at college and since to arrive where I am as a retired parish priest still doing Sunday duties for congregations eager to know their faith better. Along the way the school chaplain, an ex-Royal Marine, our Regimental Padre when I served in the army, the then Rector of my spiritual home, St. Bride's Fleet Street, Dewi Morgan, and Archbishop Stuart Blanch who ordained me, to say nothing of tutors and lecturers during my days in Oxford, studying for an MA at Hull, and since all prompted thought. If I have not made people think when taking a Sunday Service I feel I have fallen short.

My starting point has been the Revised Standard Version of the Bible that I relied on at college and since, prompted by what I remembered verbatim from the King James Authorized Version from early school days in the 1950s, and a smattering of the Greek of the original which I must confess is very rusty but useful to know the full implication of the odd word. I have also added a brief list of references to other Old Testament scripture in an index at the back per chapter relating to St. Mark's gospel for my narrative, because so much of the life and teaching of Jesus is derived from and based on the law and the prophets in the Old Testament. After all the scriptures would have been learned and familiar as the many references that can be found in Mark indicate. I have indicated where each chapter starts in my narrative and followed the flow so cross referencing the actual text in a Bible should be easy. However I hope the story itself makes plain an understanding of it from what Mark had to say being an eye witness much of the time. It can be said it is Peter's Gospel as obviously Mark must have quizzed him over the years and no doubt when prompted to write the story, perhaps by St. Paul, when they realized they were all getting older and the story needed to continue for future generations.

Introduction

Luke picks up Peter's story in Acts when Peter became a very different person, much chastened by experience, and a fervent speaker about the risen Christ and the availability of the Holy Spirit in the life of any who would genuinely seek it. This continues as another part of the Peter story by writers who obviously knew him. Where the second letter of Peter cites being at the transfiguration it adds authenticity to the letter even if not by him.

NB. I use and quote from The Revised Standard Version of the Bible which like good Yorkshire dialect retains Thee and Thou.

Part 1.

What Uncle Peter Did, as per St. Mark's Gospel

1. I UNDERSTAND ORIGINALLY Uncle Simon was minding his own business, literally, by the shore frustrated that his labours all night had been in vain. He was a fisherman. Nothing grand; just independent but prepared to join in joint efforts with friends like Zebedee and sons, James and John. That was usually seasonal depending on when a shoal formed to feed in certain areas. Also they traded together sharing an outlet in the old quarry in Jerusalem. Anyway, enough background, Uncle Simon was with his brother Andrew having another cast with their net when a stranger, gaunt like some sort of hermit, bade them follow him and catch men. Strange as the summons was who were they to take no notice? They did, and what's more, this fellow got James and John to follow him. Luckily the fishing business was not going to collapse as Zebedee always hired others and how many young men do not stay with Dad but launch out to make their own mark on the world?

It turned out that this bloke was a rabbi. He looked better after my aunt gave him a good square meal back at Uncle Simon's house in Capernaum. He was from Nazareth, called Jesus, and on the sabbath he taught in the synagogue. Not only that, but there was a man possessed there, who confronted him and knew him as

Jesus, and Jesus restored him to his right mind much to the amazement of everyone. They could not believe that he cast out unclean spirits as they saw them, but it happened before their very eyes so the news spread fast.

Anyway not only that but back at Simon's house Granny Simon as we called her had a bout of fever and Jesus restored her. Immediately she dished up some food for his gang—not a bad way to pay for a meal! Next morning I noticed he had slipped out early to pray in peace. Uncle Simon found him and wanted him to do more locally but Jesus insisted on keeping on the move and so be able to share more widely the message he had inherited from John the Baptist and developed about repentance and being in the new kingdom of God—Good News it was called. It seemed this Kingdom of God was a new Promised Land like of old to the Jewish Patriarchs but of faith and for the benefit of the soul not geophysical. It was a way to be and at one stage was later called the Way. Moreover he healed others, including a leper who implored him certain that Jesus could cure him. He did, and he even touched him to reassure him that he was clean. Usually no-one touches a leper! Jesus told him to show himself to the priest to be declared clean as the law of Moses commanded but he could not refrain from shouting out about his sudden healing so everyone began making a bee-line for Jesus who had to avoid any towns as a result.

2. It did not stop there as back in Capernaum they wanted to hear more and brought others to be healed. So much so that when the house was full of listeners, four blokes brought a paralysed man along and unable to enter stripped the roof and let him down in front of Jesus. Jesus told him his sins were forgiven which made some scribes who were there indignant because they thought it blasphemous. Realizing this Jesus set them a riddle: was it easier to forgive sins or tell him on the spot to pick up his bed and walk? So he told the man to pick up his bed and walk. He did. Jesus' healings made clear that while dis-ease of the mind may be the reward of sin not all illness or disease was caused by sin.

Part 1.

Obviously in general folk observed the sabbath and downed tools so the synagogue was a popular place if there was a good speaker and Uncle Simon said for the most part Jesus taught on the sabbath in various synagogues and people flocked to hear him as he talked sense—his was a reliable, believable and freeing Word. However this always annoyed the Pharisees as it broke their rules and contradicted their behaviour, their interpretation of the Torah, and their teaching. Jesus set no restrictions save obeying God and loving your neighbour. All very straight forward without petty rules and regulations. He even summoned Matthew to join us and leave his minding the Pharisee's cash.

3. One sabbath we went to a synagogue with him and there was a man with a withered hand. Jesus told him to stretch out his hand. The Pharisees were itching to catch him out so he asked them first 'Is it lawful on the sabbath to do good or to do harm, to save life or to kill?' He was angry at their stubbornness but they couldn't answer him. They were even more annoyed when the man's hand was restored!

We followed him back to Galilee and to the sea there where crowds came to hear him and be restored. He had to get Uncle Simon to sort out a boat so he could avoid the crush and teach from just off the shore line. Then he went up the mountain to the East and took with him those he had picked out. He chose twelve, I was too young, and sent them out to preach and gave them the authority to cast out the demons that dogged people. In naming them he renamed Uncle Simon with the nickname Peter, the Rock or Cephas in the local dialect, perhaps because he was solid and stubborn but also because he was groomed to be a foundation for the future. The others were his brother Andrew, the sons of Zebedee nicknamed The Sons of Thunder (Boanerges) who formed an inner circle with Uncle Simon or Peter as he was then known. He added Philip and Bartholomew who seemed to be chums, Matthew and Thomas the twin, James son of Alphaeus, Thadaeus (Jude), Simon the Cananaean who was a sicarii or dagger man, a zealot like Judas Iscariot who was also included to make the 12,

Uncle Peter's Story

even though he was to betray him. Somewhat eclectic it rather reflected the original twelve tribes of Israel.

This last caused some controversy as many were affected and so many were cured. His power and popularity rather disrupted life and interrupted meal times. So much so that his family wanted to drag him away even as a group from Jerusalem came down to examine him and test his orthodoxy. He gave them short shrift, pointing out that if they thought he cast out demons by the prince of demons himself then Satan would fall as it would divide his power. Rather he needed to bind Satan's power to restore normal life. He warned people not to deny the Holy Spirt at their peril. Still his family wanted to collect him but he retorted everyone was his family in what was to be a new community—the Kingdom of God where God ruled the heart and people's actions.

4. I loved his stories. Drawn from a every day life they were called parables and even then Uncle Peter and the others had to ask him to explain them. Later that day after he had told a number of parables about worth and growth in a person's response to him, and ultimately their contribution to the growth of the kingdom and its abundance, he suggested they got in a boat to cross to the other side and escape the pressure of people. A gale sprang up and it got quite rough but Jesus, worn out, was fast asleep on a cushion in the stern. Being frightened they woke him up to help with baling out the boat before it sank as he was oblivious of the danger. You can hardly imagine their amazement when he got up, rebuked the wind like he did the evil spirits and told the sea to be still. He asked them where was their faith which was difficult when he seemed to have control of the elements, indeed of creation itself.

5. Hindsight is a marvellous thing and looking back I saw things as a boy for what they were at the time when I kept Uncle Peter company and shared grown up things. Take the maniac called Legion amongst the tombs of the Gerasenes. Quite a frightening man to encounter but now I see it as a mission of Jesus to put a right spirit in people. Legion was an extreme case and Jesus

wanted, indeed told him, to stay and share his good news. Pity about the pigs but we didn't eat them then! But being considered unclean to eat it rather emphasized the parallel with a person being a reject from society with a bad spirit.

There followed another extreme case I see differently now. For a change a synagogue ruler, Jairus, sought his help! Despite interruption when a woman touched him to be healed of a 12 year hemorrhage he revived the guy's daughter, and of course she needed food. I had to stay outside but now I understand about women's monthly cycles it seems that the older woman was cured of the problems at the end of her fertility in life while the younger was struck down by the beginning of hers. Jesus had no qualms about being unclean or tainted. It was life's natural cycle affecting them. The full incident showed it was necessary to believe against or rather despite the odds. It also showed the real fertility was Jesus as the Word that brought good into the world and into people.

6. I do remember an occasion at the synagogue in his home town where people were amazed at what he taught but then thought it could not be sound as he was only the carpenter's boy. Yes, they realised Mary was his mother and the mother of not a few more children, but none of whom seemed to see him as any different from them, apart from his prophetic and rabbinical ministry as his parents had offered him to the Lord as their firstborn. Anyway as he said there was not a great deal he could do on his own doorstep as people thought they knew him too well and became sceptical.

I did not go with Uncle Peter, as he then was, when Jesus sent them out on mission in pairs and to rely on their reception wherever they went. It puzzled Herod when he heard about it all as to who Jesus was. He had beheaded John the Baptist out of pride after John reprimanded him for pinching his brother Philip's wife, Herodias. I expect they all got carried away leering at Herodias' daughter dancing so his honour and boasting had to be upheld. Anyway there was no dynastic link of Herod's family to Jesus'. Nevertheless it saddened Jesus to lose his cousin who had paved the way for him.

Uncle Peter's Story

I still puzzle that when so many people gathered round Jesus when the apostles returned from their mission that having taught them he then fed them. It was a grassy spot and sitting in companies of 50 there must have been an hundred groups of men to say nothing of the women. How 5 loaves and 2 small fishes fed so many I have no idea but 12 baskets of left-overs suggest a sufficient abundance over and above what his 12 men, good and true, did but would do more in future.

After such a feast and activity Jesus despatched the disciples by boat to Bethsaida and went into the hills to pray alone. He surprised them at 3 am when they saw him walking past like a ghost although a brisk wind was heading them and slowing their landfall. They were spooked but suddenly he was with them aboard the boat. They tied up at Gennesaret and once again Jesus was mobbed and had to heal the sick.

7. Once more I have to rely on Uncle Peter's witness of events when Jesus confronted the Pharisees with their hypocrisy. They had their view of cleanliness and washing but their laws did not encourage them to honour elderly parents, and think purer things. What you eat does not defile you but what you say might. Jesus was about seeing people had a right spirit not ticking boxes.

Wanting peace Jesus went to the seaside near Tyre and tried to hide but Uncle Peter and company could not keep folk away. Even a gentile, a Syrophoenician woman by birth, pleaded with him about her daughter. Uncle Peter says her reply brought Jesus up short. He realised he was not exclusive to the Jews as he told her; others like dogs did eat the children's crumbs under the table was her reply. She got her wish, and it must have influenced Uncle Peter when later on he was called to minister to the Gentiles in answer to Cornelius' prayers. Going along from Sidon back to Galilee in and around the Decapolis—a Gentile area—they brought a deaf man who was tongue tied to be healed so again Jesus obliged them, opened his ears and loosed his tongue. Overjoyed he could not stop himself telling everyone however much Jesus told him to keep quiet about it.

Part 1.

8. Still people flocked to feast on his words, too eager to stop and eat, but they still got hungry after 3 days. 4,000 fed this time having mustered 7 loaves and a few small fish. Even so there was plenty as they gathered 7 baskets with scraps. Nothing was wasted but it was puzzle to his friends especially as they only had one loaf between them when they got in the boat. God's creation was about abundance and if the scraps from one loaf filled a basket it struck a chord, but it was Jesus who was the true bread.

At Bethsaida Uncle Peter watched him heal a blind man. He wouldn't do it in the village but once in the outskirts he spat on the man's eyes and laid hands on him. At first as he could not figure out accurately what he saw Jesus put his hands on his eyes until he saw clearly. He told him to go home and not enter the village. He had seen Jesus.

Making for Caesarea Philippi Jesus asked his disciples 'Who do men say I am?' They replied John the Baptist, Elijah, or one of the classic prophets. A bit of a trick question as it partially answered itself we understood later. If Jews referred to God as I am who I am is not Jesus suggesting a link when he asked them 'But who do you say that I am?' Uncle Peter got it, the Christ, the one to come from God. Even though he had hit the nail on the head Jesus told him to keep quiet about it. It wasn't so much the bread but it is what Jesus feeds us. However Uncle Peter found it hard to stomach what Jesus went on to say. Referring to himself as the Son of Man, perhaps in a way a second creation of Man by God after Adam was placed in the world, he prophesied his demise at the hands of the chief priests and other Jewish authorities, after which in three days he would rise again. Uncle Peter chided him and got a stern rebuke for not rising above how men thought to focus on God's plans that Jesus represented. The Messiah that Jesus proved to be was nowhere near the Jewish expectation of a messiah whom they thought would deliver them from the Romans and restore a more perfect kingdom than David's. It was a struggle to get reality across, more so when so called leaders of the people only understood what they wanted to understand.

Jesus then went further, when a multitude gathered again with his disciples, saying about the challenge and cost of following him and sharing the enigma that if doing so for him and the gospel cost the person's life he would actually save it. It was of no value to gain the whole world at the cost of one's own life. Of those who responded now some would be alive to see this Kingdom of God that he ushered in become a reality.

9. I wish I had been there when the story that Uncle Peter narrated actually happened up a mountain, perhaps Hermon behind the source of the Jordan whose waters were the snow melt from that Mountain and akin to the waters of life flowing from a rock. Uncle Peter's description hardly does justice to the event he was so gobsmacked. Jesus took him and James and John up this high mountain where he was transfigured—there is no other word for it—before them and they saw him talking with Moses and Elijah about his exodus, his departure from the world. His clothing became gleaming white, brighter than any laundryman could manage. All Uncle Peter could manage was to blurt out something about making 3 booths—one for each of them. At that point a cloud descended and there was a voice commanding them to listen to the beloved son. The cloud cleared and there was just Jesus standing there. As Jesus said himself at other times he had not come to abolish the law (Moses) and the prophets (Elijah) but to fulfil them.

On the way down he charged them to tell no-one until he had risen from the dead which he explained to them. Then it would make sense as everything slotted into the picture and he answered their other questions saying that Elijah had already come as written and how they treated him was an indicator how the Son of Man would be treated at the mercy of men.

On joining the others it became clear they had much to learn as none of them could rid a young boy of an unclean spirit. Jesus despaired and sent for the lad, whose father begged him to restore his son. Jesus said 'All things are possible to him who believes.' The man replied very tellingly 'I believe; help my unbelief'—words that have stayed with me. Sure enough he was cured although at first everyone thought he was dead. It showed something of restoring God's glory in the world, and also serious practice of and belief in the power of prayer.

After that he wanted no distractions, only to be alone with his disciples but they could not get their heads round it with him telling them he would be betrayed and killed, yet rise after three days. They then came to Capernaum where on the strength of discussions about who was the greatest amongst them he gave them a lecture on humility to Uncle Peter's shame. His message was about serving others, receiving others, even children, which in turn was to receive Jesus. Furthermore they were not to stop those who might heal in Jesus' name because they must surely work for him and will receive their reward. Uncle Peter remembered that Jesus' teaching could use extreme metaphors to make a point that was not to be taken lightly but also not literally! The disciples were to be the salt that seasoned the whole, a living sacrifice if needs be. If salt loses its saltness it is no use but they would eventually be salted with Holy Spirit and burn with ardour to proclaim the Good News.

10. Jesus took his disciples further afield and taught the crowds that gathered beyond the Jordan. Inevitably the Pharisees came and tried to catch him out asking about divorce. Typically he turned the question back on them 'What did Moses command?' To their reply he added Moses did allow it as they answered but only because of their stubbornness. Furthermore God made male and female, dividing Adam to make Eve, so once joined in marriage they become one flesh again and completed the cycle God started in dividing Adam to make Eve; therefore man should not put asunder what God has joined. Divorcing is the root of adultery he told the disciples later and where the law gets broken.

During a lull people brought children to be blessed by Jesus but Uncle Peter recalled Jesus got indignant with the disciples when they shooed them away for they illustrated that those who did not receive the Kingdom of God with a childlike trust and acceptance would never enter it. The disciples, and especially Uncle Peter, learned many lessons of the Lord the hard way!

And hard it was for a young man who wanted to inherit that asset of the Kingdom of God—eternal life. No doubt he thought it living forever enjoying his wealth but he slunk away when Jesus talked of giving his wealth away and enjoying the wealth of the Kingdom. At one stage even Jesus was hopeful because he assiduously kept the commandments, but, alas, he was too tied to possessions. Jesus remarked, which many well remember, that it was easier for a camel to pass through the eye of a needle than for a rich man to enter the Kingdom of God. It appeared that entrance was therefore difficult for everyone so Uncle Peter remonstrated, saying his disciples had left everything to follow him. Jesus replied the rewards would follow to repay the cost of the gospel and in the age to come would be eternal life.

Setting off for Jerusalem he repeated that there he would be betrayed to the chief priests, condemned by the Roman authorities, abused and killed, but rise after three days. This suggestion of the end being near prompted James and John to seek a favour and sit either side of him in his glory. He asked them if the were able to share his cup and his baptism? They said they were able. Jesus replied they would but it was beyond him to grant their request, which made the other ten indignant with them. Calming the situation Jesus reminded them that greatness came with service to others, for he, as the Son of Man, came not to be served but to serve and give his life as a ransom for many.

As they left Jericho a blind beggar, Bartimaeus the son of Timaeus, was waiting by the roadside and holla-ed after them calling on Jesus to have mercy on him. The more he was told to shut it the louder he shouted. Eventually Jesus stopped and said to call him. When he approached Jesus asked him what he wanted and he replied 'Master, let me receive my sight.' Jesus told him to go his way for blind faith had restored him. Able at last to see he followed Jesus on the way.

11. Near Jerusalem at Bethphage and Bethany, at the Mount of Olives, he told two disciples to go into the village opposite and collect a donkey, an unbroken colt, for him. If anyone asked they

Part 1.

were to reply that the Lord had need of it. It was so. When they brought the colt to Jesus they put their garments on it before Jesus got on. Thus he entered Jerusalem with the crowds spreading leafy branches before him and their garments on the road, shouting their praises and their joy "Hosanna! Blessed is he who comes in the name of the Lord! Blessed is the kingdom of our father David that is coming! Hosanna in the highest!" It was straight out of Isaiah 62, v11, as if the words of the prophet had come to life. In Jerusalem Jesus looked round the temple and went out to Bethany with the twelve to where Lazarus and his sisters lived.

Next day feeling hungry as they returned from Bethany Jesus saw a fig tree but, despite the leaves, there was nothing on it. It was not the season for figs. In the hearing of those with him he cursed it 'May no-one ever eat fruit from you again.' It was ominous as obviously being a symbol of Israel which was run by the man-made laws of the Pharisees there was better fruit to be had in what he taught. With hindsight it was as if the fruit on the tree stolen by Adam and Eve that led to disaster was replaced by the fruit of the cross—his body and blood in the bread and wine of the last supper—that led to life.

Jesus entered the temple and went riot driving out those selling and buying, overturning the tables of money changers and those selling pigeons for sacrifices at inflated exchange rates for shekels, and blocked those laden from taking a short cut through the temple. He shouted out 'Is it not written "My house shall be called a house of prayer for all nations?" But ye have made it a den of thieves.' It recalled the words of Jeremiah castigating those in God's name who abused and debased the sanctity of the temple. He amazed the multitude but annoyed the chief priests who looked for a way to be rid of him.

Returning the following morning Uncle Peter remembered what Jesus had said when they saw the fig tree he had cursed had withered away. Jesus likened it to the power of prayer and belief in God. Ask and believe you have received it. However if you have anything against anyone forgive, then our Father who is in heaven may forgive us our trespasses.

Uncle Peter's Story

Back in the temple the chief priests and their crowd asked him by what authority he taught and acted? As ever he retorted with a question about whether the baptism of John was heaven sent or devised by men? Arguing amongst themselves they could not decide since they were trapped either way: if of heaven why did they not believe, but if devised by men that denied the real and recognised prophetic ministry of John. Jesus would not tell them as even the blind could see that either way it came from God direct or through John.

12. Uncle Peter has a more vivid memory of the events that followed and I, too, was more there than not. It started with some intense teaching and confrontation with the Pharisees and others in authority. He really annoyed them when he told a parable that even they knew that it criticized them. A man planned a proper vineyard and when he had finished let it out and travelled afar. In due course when harvest came he sent a servant to collect some of the fruit, but the tenants abused him and chucked him out. He sent several others whom they treated the same and even killed some. Eventually he sent his only son reasoning that they would respect him. But no, seeing the heir had come they killed him so they would get the vineyard. Jesus implied that what they rejected was the foundation stone for something new. They would be swept away as surely as the vineyard owner would sweep the dishonest tenants away. Slowly Jesus' story made more sense for Uncle Peter and for the disciples.

Back came the Pharisees and some Herodians to trap him with a trick question about paying taxes to Caesar or not? Aware of their hypocrisy he asked for a coin and then showing them the head asked whose head and inscription was it? They replied it was Caesar's. He dumbfounded them with his reply 'Then render to Caesar the things that are Caesar's and to God things that are God's.' Who could forget the truth behind his reply?

Since Jesus had talked about rising after three days he was obviously talking about resurrection, so unsurprisingly along came the Sadducees with a trick question as they did not believe in the resurrection. Being doctors of the law they quoted Moses' ruling that if a married man died without children his brother took his widow as wife to raise children to her late husband. Thus if a man died who had six brothers and each had her in turn as wife before they died but without raising any children whose wife of the seven brothers would she be in the resurrection? Jesus chided them for neither knowing the scriptures nor the power of God, for there is no marriage in heaven. Anyway as God said to Moses that he was the God of Abraham, and the God of Isaac, and the God of Jacob so therefore he was the God of the living not the dead.

At this point a scribe came to quiz him hearing their dispute and asked which commandment was the first of all? Jesus replied with the Shema, 'The first commandment is that: The Lord our God is one Lord and thou shalt love the Lord thy God with all thy heart, with all thy soul, with all thy mind and with thy strength' and went on with the second "You shall love your neighbour as yourself." The scribe's reply in turn chimed in with what Jesus taught that God is one, and to love Him with all human emotion was a true answer along with loving one's neighbour. Obedience to these was a far greater sacrifice than burnt offerings. Jesus acknowledged that this scribe was not far from the Kingdom of God.

Jesus then posed his own riddle about the scribes saying that the if Christ is the son of David how could they believe it when he quoted from the Psalms that David himself inspired by the Holy Spirit said "The Lord said unto my Lord: Sit at my right hand till I put thy enemies under thy feet." If David therefore called him Lord how could he be his son? And he issued a warning to the crowd to beware of the scribes who made an ostentatious display of their faith and prayers, and swallowed widows' houses as tithes. At which point he sat down opposite the treasury and observed a poor widow putting in a penny as opposed to large amounts by the rich. He remarked that she put in far more than they because they could afford it.

13. On leaving the temple one of the disciples drew his attention to the fine stonework of Herod's builders. Jesus replied that

they would be torn down. On the Mount of Olives opposite Uncle Peter and James and John asked him on the side when such things would happen? Jesus replied to beware of false prophets claiming to be him. Life would still have its ups and downs, for wars and natural disasters for a start would continue to happen. As for them be prepared as to preach the gospel would cause them to be arrested and to suffer punishment, albeit undeserved. As it is, he went on to say, not to worry how you answer your accusers as the Holy Spirit will give you utterance, even when family betray you. Also that when you see another sacrilegious statue set up in the temple precinct like Antiochus Epiphanes, referred to since as 'the abomination that makes desolate', take to the hills for safety for tribulation will follow. The timing is God's but there will still be false Christs. It is another apocalypse. The heavens will change before the Son of Man returns to summon his chosen. Watch the signs of the times for just as you see a fig tree in first leaf you know that summer follows. Watch as only the Father knows the day and the hour. Watch like a doorkeeper who has no idea when his master will return but he must be awake and prepared. Watch, wait, and be ready was the clue.

14. We were aware that the chief priests were out to arrest Jesus but they feared to do so during the Passover because of a likely reaction of the crowds who flocked to him. So it was that Jesus dined with Simon the Leper in Bethany. In came a woman with an alabaster jar of pure nard, of no small value, which she broke and poured over Jesus' head. The mean spirited thought it a waste at the expense of the poor but Jesus intervened and let her be, saying that there were always poor about whom one could help any time when one wanted, but he was not always going to be there. It was a beautiful gesture and she had anointed him before he was to be buried. It, and indeed she herself, would be forever part of his story. At this point Judas Iscariot went out to see the chief priests and arrange to betray Jesus to them for a fee.

So as the Passover approached on the first day of unleavened bread when the passover lamb was sacrificed the disciples asked

Part 1.

Jesus where they might go and prepare for him to eat the passover? He told them to go into the city and when they encountered a man carrying a water jar to follow him and ask the householder where he went about the guest room, bearing in mind it was unusual for a man to carry a water jar unless he was a boy helping out as it was woman's work. It was as he said and they were shown a large upper room suitably prepared. That evening he came with the twelve and were surprised during the meal when he said one of them would betray him. They quizzed each other but Jesus assured them that one of them would betray him as it was foretold about the Son of Man but woe betide that person.

Then he took bread during the meal, broke it after giving thanks, and gave it to them saying within my hearing as I was serving 'Take; eat this is my body.' Then he took a cup of wine, gave thanks, and gave it to them to drink again saying words that have remained ever since 'This is my blood of the covenant which is poured out for many,' adding that he would not drink of the fruit of the vine until the day that he drank it new in the Kingdom of God. They sang an hymn and went out to the Mount of Olives. Jesus warned them that they would fall away as, quoting Zechariah the prophet "I will strike the shepherd, and the sheep will be scattered." But there was hope since when he was raised up they would find him in Galilee.

Uncle Peter swore blind that even if they all fell away he would not. Jesus bluntly replied 'In truth I tell you, even tonight before the cock crows twice thou shalt deny me thrice.' Uncle Peter would have none of it and that even to death he would not deny Jesus.

They went to a garden called Gethsemane and Jesus bade his disciples to sit and wait while he prayed further on. He took with him Uncle Peter, James and John but he was very agitated. He said he was full of sorrow, his soul distressed to death, and bade them watch and wait. Further on he fell on the ground and prayed to be spared the next hour. I followed quietly and heard him pray 'Father, with thee all things are possible; remove this cup from me; nevertheless not my will be done but thine.' He returned and found them asleep, saying to Uncle Peter 'What Simon, you asleep? Could you not keep watch for an hour? Watch and pray that you are not led into temptation; the spirit is indeed willing but weak indeed is the flesh.' Twice more he went and made the same prayer only to return and find them asleep. After returning the third time he woke them up and urged that they should go for the hour had come for the Son of Man, as he referred to himself, was about to be betrayed to sinners, and his betrayer was at hand.

At this point Judas appeared with an armed gang from the chief priests, scribes and elders. He kissed Jesus as that was the sign he had given them as to whom they should arrest, saying "Master!" The armed crowd seized him, but someone following Jesus had a sword and struck out cutting the ear of the high priest's servant. Jesus chided them for coming out bristling with arms as if to arrest a robber, when any day previously they could have arrested him in the temple as he taught, but the scriptures had to be fulfilled and his followers fled. I was there following clothed in a linen cloth, but when they grabbed me I cast it off and fled naked.

Uncle Peter followed at a distance when they took Jesus to the high priest and his colleagues and entered the courtyard to sit with the guards and warm himself at the fire.

I expect he overheard some of the goings on as they accused Jesus but could come up with nothing concrete, contradicting each other. Some bore false witness claiming to hear him say that he would destroy the temple made with hands and build another in three days not made with hands. Nothing stuck. When the high priest demanded an answer Jesus remained silent. The high priest then asked "Are you the Christ, the Son of the Blessed?" Jesus answered 'I am (the first half of the Hebrew name for God that was never uttered); and you will see the Son of Man seated at the right hand of Power, and coming with the clouds of heaven.' In a rage the high priest tore his garments shouting "blasphemy" and saying that all must have heard and no further witness was needed so what did they say? They condemned him to death and abused him, spitting and hitting and demanding he prophesy. The guards roughly manhandled him away.

Part 1.

Meanwhile in the courtyard Uncle Peter was quizzed, first by one of the high priest's maids that he was from Nazarus and was with Jesus. He denied it 'I neither know nor understand what you mean.' With that he went to the gateway. She saw him again and said to the bystanders 'This man is one of them.' Again Peter denied it. But eventually the bystanders said 'Certainly you are one of them, for by your accent you are a Galilean.' Uncle Peter invoked a curse on himself swearing 'I don't know this man you speak about.' Immediately a cock crowed a second time and Uncle Peter remembered how Jesus had chided him. He was reduced to tears.

15. In the morning after a consultation all the chief priests and others bound Jesus and took him off to Pilate, who asked him if he was the King of the Jews? Jesus' replied 'So you say.' The chief priests butted in with accusations and Pilate asked him if he had an answer to so many accusations but Jesus remained silent which caused Pilate to wonder.

At the feast it was customary to pardon a prisoner or robber for whom people asked and amongst the rebels held in prison was Barabbas—son of the father—who was notorious, a robber, who had committed murder in a recent insurrection against the Romans. The crowd approached asking expecting Pilate to honour the custom and asked him to release someone. He asked if they might want the King of the Jews? He knew the malice of the chief priests but they prompted the crowd to shout for Barabbas. Pilate then asked "Then what about the King of the Jews?' They replied 'Crucify him.' Pilate responded 'But what evil has he done?' but they chanted 'Crucify him.' To satisfy the crowd and prevent any hostility he released Barabbas, (since Jesus was also referred to as the Son of the Father perhaps some thought they shouted for him?). Pilate had Jesus scourged and delivered him to be crucified.

The soldiers led Jesus into the praetorium and called together the whole battalion who clothed him with a purple cloak, plaited a crown of thorns and placed it on his head, saluting him and then mocked, hit, and spat at him. It was a chance to mock the Jews so 'Hail, King of the Jews!' they cried. Stripping the cloak from him

Uncle Peter's Story

they returned his clothes and led him out for crucifixion. The treatment much weakened Jesus so they compelled Simon of Cyrene who was passing to carry Jesus' cross. This Simon had come in from the country and was the father of Alexander and Rufus, all of whom were to play a part in the early church as it evolved.

They brought Jesus to Golgotha, known as the place of a skull, and offered him wine made bitter with myrrh, but he refused it, although intended as pain relief. Having nailed him to a cross and erected it they divided his clothes, casting lots for what each should have. It was the third hour. The charge against him was written down and displayed "The King of the Jews." Two robbers were crucified with him, one on either side. Passersby mocked him, taunting him with the claim to destroy the temple and build it in three days. So too the chief priests and scribes "He saved others, why not himself? Come down from the cross then we shall believe." It was like the temptations he had faced in the wilderness all over again.

At the sixth hour it went dark until the ninth hour when Jesus then cried out 'Eloi, Eloi, lama sabachthani?' (My God, my God, why hast thou forsaken me?') Some thought he was summoning Elijah, others offered on a reed a sponge dipped in vinegar for him. Jesus then uttered a loud cry and breathed his last. Amazingly at the same time it was discovered that the curtain in the temple that screened off the Holy of Holies was torn from above, from top to bottom, as if to let in the light and expose its emptiness against only the high priest entering once a year. Perhaps it mirrored the empty tomb three days later and what it said about the presence of God in a new light. Even the centurion commanding the guard, standing opposite as he expired, was moved saying 'Truly this man was the Son of God!'

That very evening since it was the day of Preparation before the sabbath one man, Joseph of Arimathea and a respected council member but also searching for the Kingdom of God, courageously begged Pilate for Jesus' body. Pilate was amazed that Jesus had already died and summoned the centurion to check. When he in turn confirmed it Pilate gave the OK to Joseph who took a linen

Part 1.

shroud to wrap the body when he had taken Jesus down. He laid him in a new tomb hewn from the rock and rolled a stone across the entrance. I saw Mary Magdalen and Mary the mother of Joses looking where Jesus was laid.

16. With the sabbath over Mary Magdalen and Mary the mother of James, and Salome brought spices to the tomb to anoint him, at dawn literally as the sun rose on the first day of the week. Of course they wondered who would roll back the stone for them, especially as it was very large, but they found it already done on arrival. Entering the tomb they saw a young man in a white robe sitting on the right side. He spoke to them 'Do not be amazed; you seek Jesus of Nazareth, who was crucified. He has risen, he is not here; see the place where they laid him. But go, tell his disciples and Peter that he is going before you to Galilee; there you will see him, as he told you.' The women went out and fled, overcome and baffled. They did not say anything to anyone for they were afraid.

16, verses 9–11 or verses 9–20 are an epilogue that put the first part of the chapter in different lights. Was the young man Mark himself who had followed at a distance from the beginning and observed so much? Or was the young man in a white robe representing those dressed and presented for baptism and stating a mini-creed that Jesus was dead, buried and risen? Or is it a sudden end to leave the reader to draw his own conclusions to say 'I believe, help thou my unbelief'? A challenge to believe when ironically this and the added narrative tells us that those who first witnessed the empty tomb and the resurrection were not believed!

Some texts add verses 9–11 as an obvious epilogue to round off the story with hindsight:
But they reported briefly to Peter and those with him all that they had been told. And after this, Jesus himself sent out by means of them, from east to west, the sacred and imperishable proclamation of eternal salvation.

Uncle Peter's Story

Most Bibles contain the usual fuller epilogue as well, verses 9–20:

> Now when Jesus rose on the first day of the week he appeared first to Mary Magdalen from whom he had cast out seven demons. She went to tell those who had been with him as they mourned and wept. When she told them they would not believe it. He then appeared to two of them as they returned to the country [Emmaus—see Luke 24, verses 13—35, which point to a later addition] from Jerusalem, who hastened back to tell the others who would still not believe them.
>
> Afterwards as the eleven ate he appeared to them and upbraided them for their unbelief and hardness of heart, and for failing to believe them who had seen him after he had risen. He commissioned them 'Go into all the world and preach the gospel to the whole creation. He who believes and is baptized will be saved; but he who does not believe will be condemned. And these signs shall accompany those who believe: in my name they shall cast out evil spirits; they will speak in new tongues; they will pick up serpents, and if they drink any deadly thing, it will not hurt them*; they will lay their hands on the sick. and they will recover.'
>
> So after the Lord has spoken to them he was taken up into heaven at sat down at God's right hand. So they went out and preached everywhere while the Lord worked with them and confirmed the message by the signs that attended it. Amen.**

*Some are known to take these two phrases literally, even a test of faith, but more likely it refers to false Christs who would seduce like the serpent in the garden of Eden and to false communion that is poisonous in intention by resembling true communion. In other words beware of opposition dressed up as the real thing.

**This addition is worth comparing with Matthew 28 and Luke 24, vv36–49, along with John 20.

Part 2.

Peter as John heard through the eyes and ears of St. John's Gospel

WHEN JOHN WAS WRITING his memory of Uncle Peter I was elsewhere having been useful to Paul and travelled with him and Barnabas until we went our separate ways and I returned with the latter to Cyprus, (Acts 15, vv36–41). Of course time and memory may distort facts and even through being relayed through different people will cause some fluctuations to the details and how the story is received. So maybe as John says Uncle Peter came into contact with Jesus through Andrew as he was fishing, (1, v40) and was then, verse 42, nicknamed Cephas.

As an eyewitness like John let me reserve my comments to what John wrote that I did not see or, indeed, understand being a youngster at the time. When Jesus declared himself 'I am the bread of life' (6,v48) many could not stomach it. It was better than the old manna from heaven as his flesh in the form of bread would sustain life, but spiritual life is what Jesus meant. Prophetic poetry might often appear as a riddle to those who could not grasp the point but Uncle Peter got what the point was and was not going to withdraw from Jesus (6, v68), these were words of eternal life and sustenance.

As a demonstration of service to others and refraining from lording it over others Jesus washed the feet of the disciples at the

Uncle Peter's Story

Last Supper as it came to be known. Uncle Peter, impetuous as ever, (13, v6ff) expostulated; first refusing to be washed and then demanding to be washed all over because he could not grasp the symbolism of the action. Then during the meal when Jesus indicated that one of the disciples would betray him Uncle Peter was curious to know who would so he nudged the disciple close to Jesus physically and emotionally to ask him (13, v24) and Jesus replied it was the one to whom he gave a morsel from the meal after he had dipped it. Significantly it was bread that in a sense was contaminated by other food, indeed earthly. It was given to Judas, whom, I may say, no-one really trusted. John tells us that it was Uncle Peter, when Jesus was betrayed and arrested, who drew a sword in defence and struck the high priest's slave cutting off his ear (Luke says Jesus healed it!). 18, v11 John records Jesus said 'Put up your sword in its sheath; shall I not drink the cup the Father has given me?' Compare the reference to the cup with Jesus' earlier prayer in Gethsemane as recorded in Mark 14, vv32-42 and the two other synoptic gospels.

Then when Jesus announced his departure, exodus, impending as it turned out from the world, Uncle Peter was curious to know where? (13, v36-37). When Jesus told him he could not follow him immediately Uncle Peter was perplexed and vowed to die for him, only to be rebuked that he would deny Jesus three times that very night, which he did in the court of the high priest (18, vv15-18, 25-27) almost on cue which cut him up when he realised. Could he ever make up for such a betrayal?

As it turned out he was restored to favour and future evangelism in a roundabout and unexpected way. When the women found the tomb was empty on the third day after Jesus had been crucified and told Uncle Peter and the others (20,vv1-10) two of them ran to the tomb. The 'other' disciple, who outran Uncle Peter, also could be understood as the 'brother' disciple, which could indicate Andrew. It was one thing to find the empty tomb, but totally another to believe that Mary Magdalen had seen him until he appeared to them even though they were locked in an upper

PART 2.

room that same evening. It turned out though that Thomas was elsewhere so missed out and remained incredulous.

(Chapter 21). Some time after Jesus had appeared to them 8 days after his first appearance Uncle Peter felt it was time to return to everyday life and with 6 of the others went fishing back in the Sea of Galilee at Tiberius. They laboured all night in vain. A figure on the shore in the morning asked if they had caught anything and when they replied 'No' he said to cast their net on the other side. The net was overwhelmed! The disciple who was close to Jesus at the last supper and was fishing with them realised who it was and said to Uncle Peter 'It's the Lord!' Covering himself Uncle Peter leapt ashore and left the others to haul the nets.

On shore already cooking were some grilled fish and some bread. They were bidden to breakfast and Jesus fed them. It was the third time they had encountered him after finding the tomb empty.

After breakfast the Lord grilled Uncle Peter and asked him three times if he loved him which began to pain him. Each time Uncle Peter confessed his love and in response the Lord gave him a commandment to Feed my lambs, tend my sheep, and feed my sheep. In the light of day when Jesus appears to him, no longer by night in Jerusalem, Uncle Peter is forgiven and restored and given a new commission to be a shepherd of people. It might well take him where he would rather not go; it might well cost him his life at the hands of others; nevertheless the command from the risen Lord was 'Follow me!' It would turn out to be literally in Uncle Peter's case.

POSTSCRIPT:

Inevitably Peter was curious about what was of no concern to him— the fate of that disciple who was close to Jesus. All were close, but of John, Lazarus, and Andrew, who in particular might be singled out perhaps never to die? John had been entrusted with Mary the Mother of Jesus. Lazarus had died once already! Andrew often seemed to be at hand with a ready answer; finding his brother to begin with;

finding some food to feed a multitude; recognizing Jesus when they caught a shoal of fishes. Was there a special task to remain to do until Jesus came since he had at one stage shared Jesus' confidence about the signs of the times? (Mark 13, v3.) Jesus mentioned the hour had come (John12. vv22ff) when he and Philip went to tell Jesus there were some Greeks wanting to see him.

Again if the brother disciple outran Uncle Peter, and believed when he saw how the empty tomb was inside when he went in, it was appropriate to following Jesus in a new light. It can be noted that when Jesus ordered Lazarus to come forth (John 11, vv38–44) from the tomb he commanded he should be unbound from his grave clothes yet John tells us Jesus' grave clothes were folded neatly and the napkin that had covered his face rolled up separately (John 20, vv6–20.) Hence this close disciple responding to Jesus in belief would suggest a new lease of life, the eternal life of the Kingdom of God rather than not physically dying as some understood.

A further take on the disciple whom Jesus loved is that it is the reader. All are close to the Lord at the communion table. Who knows who might betray, or deny as we would say post resurrection, the Lord in our own time? Although outrunning Peter it is Peter who takes the first step and afterwards takes the lead. The other disciple, as stated, sees and believes despite the emptiness of the tomb which equates with our own experience. We can only accept the emptiness of the tomb that all the Gospels describe as a fact of our Christian faith. Lastly when Jesus is quizzed by Peter about this other disciple it can refer to those of us in our own time, day and age who come to belief because we all remain until we take Jesus on board.

Part 3.

St. Matthew on Peter

MATTHEW IS THE MOST Jewish of the Gospels and was written for the benefit of the Jews where many references to the Old Testament show that Jesus fulfilled these prophecies. It also shows where his teaching did not abolish the law and the prophets but fulfilled them in a new Way to be centred on loving one's neighbour as oneself. There are 3 points of focus on Peter: his impetuous desire to walk on the water from a storm tossed boat to Jesus nearby 14, vv28–33; his confession 16, vv13–20; and on forgiveness 18, vv21–35. The latter two both mention the church which suggests a later gospel when the church was established in Jerusalem and Peter her main advocate. The first is twofold: a character sketch of Peter who, by the time the gospel was written, was or had been (if already executed) a leader and founder of the church and secondly a reminder that while Peter's embryo faith failed him it is firm belief that buoys people up.

Of the first reference by Matthew to the church following Simon Peter's confession and recognition that Jesus is the Christ Jesus calls petros, Peter, and says that "on this rock, petra, I will build my church that death cannot destroy." Jesus continues that "I will give you the keys of the kingdom of heaven that whatever you bind on earth shall have been bound in heaven and whatever you loose on earth shall be loosed in heaven." Thus as the Church evolved she had the authority to forgive or not forgive. A potent power that the Inquisitions and Star Chambers of the late middle ages clearly abused and hindered rather than grew the Church.

In Matthew's second reference there was the important question of forgiveness stemming from a question asked by Peter following the section by Matthew on Church discipline. Jesus' parable, 18, vv23–35 endorses forgiveness as in the Lord's prayer (debts in Matthew and Scotland!) 6, vv9–13 being conditional on our forgiving others. In fact despite rules and regulations if Jesus is followed as he lived and taught all these disciplines become self regulating and we as individuals avoid judgement.

It is worth adding that if Matthew's gospel is considered later than Mark, but drawing on some of the same source or on it as source, the references to the early church as it formed suggest that some sort of formula around the Christian faith was forming in relation to Jesus' commission at the end of the gospel, 28, v19, 'Go therefore and make disciples of all nations, baptizing them in the name of the Father and of the Son and of the Holy Spirit. . .' It is the first mention of a Trinity. Whilst later Creeds centre on the Trinity they contain little gospel narrative and were devised to recite a common orthodoxy formalizing a common belief. The Nicene Creed, formulated at the Council of Nicaea, 325 AD, laid a basic structure. The Apostles' Creed, dated as we know it 390 AD was probably based on an oral tradition used at Baptisms from as early as 150 AD but formalized in the 4th Century and later included in the daily office of the Western Church, especially the Book of Common Prayer, 1662 as we have it. 381–428 AD saw a third Creed in the Western Church, the Athanasian Creed focussed more on the Trinity and Incarnation, but certainly not written by Saint Athanasius who lived 396–473 AD.

Part 4.

Uncle Peter's activities as recorded by Luke in The Acts of the Apostles

AFTER PENTECOST UNCLE PETER had a new confidence and authority in his faith and took on a new lease of life full of zeal for the risen Christ. I saw less of him as he went about preaching this good news, but Luke caught up with him and included a full account of his activities when he wrote up the aftermath of Pentecost following our Lord's Ascension and physical exodus from the world.

1, (v13–15). After Jesus was taken up, having told the disciples to wait until they were baptized with fire—the Holy Spirit—they returned to Jerusalem where they had an Upper Room and focused on prayer along with the women of their company, Jesus' Mother, Mary, and his brothers. It was Uncle Peter who proposed electing another from the growing company to replace Judas to restore their number as close disciples to twelve. After casting lots for the two selected candidates, Joseph Barsabbas, known as Justus, and Matthias, the lot fell on the latter and he was enrolled with the eleven apostles as they came to be known—first hand witnesses.

2, (v13–38). On the day of Pentecost—50 days after the Passover had been celebrated—when all were gathered together they received a baptism of fire, like tongues of flame on each, and they began to explain the good news in many different languages and dialects as the Spirit loosed their tongues. At the time Jerusalem was filled with other Jews from all over, from Asia Minor and further afield from the African coast who were amazed to hear these Galileans describe the recent mighty works of God in their own language so they could understand. Mind you there were also scoffers saying they were drunk!

At this Uncle Peter rose to his feet and preached a sermon, stating that so early in the day they were not drunk or intoxicated with spirit but full of Holy Spirit as Joel had prophesied. It was indeed the Day of the Lord and salvation awaited anyone who called upon His name. He told them how Jesus, whose mighty wonders many had witnessed was cancelled and killed by men beyond the law, but God raised him up as death could not hold him, quoting David as from Psalm 16, vv8–11 referencing David's vision of the Lord before him, and Psalm 110 quoting God speaking of God the Son, or Messiah as we would understand it. David died and his tomb remains, for he has not ascended to heaven like Jesus though not abandoned in Hades but it is Jesus who is commanded to sit at the Lord's right hand—God's right hand. God has made this crucified Jesus both Lord and Christ and the psalmist's prophecy is fulfilled or we can see it another way that it is now revealed how we understand what the psalmist wrote.

This put all who heard in a flutter and they asked the twelve what should they do? There was a full response to the twelve's reply 'Repent, and be baptized every one of you in the name of Jesus Christ for the forgiveness of your sins; and you shall receive the gift of the Holy Spirit.' About three thousand were baptized and followed the apostles enjoying their teaching, fellowship, and communion. And so a community of believers sprang up holding many things in common and sharing all that they had.

3. Uncle Peter preached again in the temple when he and John went up to the temple for evening prayer. A lame man used to be left at the Beautiful Gate to beg and asked for alms from them. Uncle Peter fixed him with his gaze saying 'Silver and gold

Part 4.

have I none, but that which I have I will give you; in the name of Jesus Christ of Nazareth, walk' and took his right hand to raise him up. Restored to his feet he leaped about praising God and followed them to the amazement of all who had seen it happen. This caused more people to crowd round so Uncle Peter had to explain. He said that even amongst those who witnessed this man's restoration to his feet there were some who had shouted down Pilate when he offered to release Jesus so they were guilty of killing the Author of Life. But God had it otherwise and raised him from the dead which his disciples witnessed and therefore it is faith in this name that makes these things possible and has restored this man's health.

Uncle Peter continued, saying that people had acted in ignorance, but had not God foretold through the prophets that his Christ should suffer and resurrect? Repentance was called for to turn back to this Jesus and be refreshed by his name, since all that was foretold has come to pass and now is the chance to find blessing and forgiveness.

4. At this point the priests, the temple authorities, and the Sadducees (who do not hold with resurrection) had them arrested and put in custody for teaching the people and proclaiming in Jesus the resurrection of the dead.

The next day Uncle Peter and John were brought before all the rulers, elders, scribes and the high priests with their family (in effect the Jerusalem aristocracy) who were gathered together and asked them by what power or by what name had they done the healing?

Uncle Peter did not hold back and plainly explained that in the name of Jesus Christ of Nazareth, whom they had crucified but whom God had raised from the dead, was the man able to stand before them. Jesus was the key stone that you builders of faith rejected but is now the very foundation stone of belief. There is no salvation in anyone else, nor in any other name under heaven to save us all.

Recognizing that they had been with Jesus and unable to deny the lame man, even though over 40, had been healed the authorities called them back and forbade them to teach in the name of or use the name of Jesus. Uncle Peter and John got proper indignant and demanded of them whether before God himself they should listen to them or to God as they could only speak the truth of what they had witnessed? They turfed the two out because they knew they could give them no other punishment because of all the people and the praise being given by them in turn to God for the healing that had been engendered.

When the two returned to the brethren and gave an account of their experience they gave praise as one and prayed noting that again prophecy was fulfilled as the authorities raged in their blindness. So they prayed for greater power to do the work of Jesus, acknowledging like a formula that God had intended the life, death, and release of power in Jesus' name all along, and the Holy Spirit came mightily upon them.

So it was that the community grew and began to hold things in common and to share. One Joseph, known as Barnabas (Son of encouragement), in fact a Levite from Cyprus, sold some land and brought the money to the apostles for the common good.

5. Amongst others who followed this example to fund the early church, as it became known, was a couple, Ananias and Sapphira, who together sold a property for the common good but connived to withhold some of the value. When Uncle Peter confronted him with his intentions and lies he dropped dead. No sooner had those who buried him returned than they had his wife to bury for she too dropped dead when Uncle Peter pointed out the discrepancy of their story and their cheating. So it became a warning to all to be honest and conceal nothing from the Holy Spirit.

Such was Uncle Peter's reputation that the number who believed his message grew and many brought many more to him to be healed even if only his shadow could cross them. At this the temple authorities and chief priests were filled with jealousy and had the apostles arrested and thrown in the common prison. By some miracle they were let out and told to go and speak the words of this new Eternal Life in the temple which they did at daybreak.

Part 4.

This much perplexed the chief priests to be told they were not in prison despite locked doors but teaching in the temple. So the captain of the guard and his men discreetly brought them to the high priests and council to avoid angering the people and getting stoned themselves. There they were told they had been forbidden to teach in Jesus' name and it appears that now they would besmirch the council and chief priests for murdering Jesus. Uncle Peter and the apostles made a clear reply that was written down 'We must obey God rather than men. The God of our fathers raised Jesus whom you killed by hanging him on a tree. God exalted him to his right hand on high as Leader and Saviour, to give repentance to Israel and forgiveness of sins. And we are witnesses to these things, and so is the Holy Spirit whom God has given to those who obey him.' The very argument that Jesus had with the temple authorities about obeying God or their interpretation of the laws raged on!

At this their accusers were even more enraged and wanted to kill them. At this point a Pharisee called Gamaliel gave then wise counsel. He pointed out that previous movements had failed and their followers scattered on the death of their leaders, so take note: if these doings are of God let them alone and do not oppose God, but if these doings are of men they will fizzle out. So the apostles were beaten and thrown out, charged to keep silent, but they were in the temple all the more preaching Jesus was the Christ.

6. Although not mentioned by name Uncle Peter obviously took the lead and so the church began to grow in structure, outreach, and authority. (Often where the disciples had been mentioned as a body and now as apostles it should be understood that Peter was party to the goings on.) When a certain rift was brewing between orthodox Jews and those who accepted Greek culture and language over the latter's widows missing out on the daily distribution the Apostles decided to appoint deacons to serve at tables to free themselves to preach the Word. Of the seven appointed the foremost in witness and work was one called Stephen. With more witnesses to speak and work the word of God increased so did the number of believers—even some of the priests! Great was Stephen's

eloquence and he achieved much amongst the people with signs and wonders, and when the synagogue of the Freedmen disputed with him he spoke such wisdom with the Spirit that they made no headway with their arguments and resolved to shop him to the council. They instigated false witnesses to say he would change the customs that Moses had handed down.

7. Once arrested Stephen was brought before the council and quizzed whether what his detractors said was true? In his defence he pointed to the history of Israel as recorded in the scriptures—their own background and Jesus'. Two people chosen by God saved the Israelites, Joseph and Moses, yet both were quizzed and doubted by their fellows 'Who made you judge over us?' Despite his wonders to release them from Egypt the Israelites forsook Moses' teaching in his absence and set up an idol angering God. In the wilderness they had the tent of witness, and once settled in the promised land by David it was Solomon, not David, who built the temple under God's directions as indeed had the tent been before in the desert. He reminded them that God had said he does not dwell in houses made by men but in all creation. Then he told them how obstinate they were to resist the Holy Spirit like their forefathers who had persecuted the prophets because their words had not tallied with their own thoughts about the coming of the Righteous One, whom they, in turn, betrayed and murdered despite receiving the law which they had failed to keep.

At his words they were all enraged, more so when Stephen described his vision of the Son of Man standing at the right hand of God. In many ways it followed the death of Jesus as they rushed on him, threw him out of the city and stoned him. So Stephen became the first martyr, praying 'Lord Jesus, receive my spirit.' Kneeling he cried out 'Lord. lay not this sin to their charge.' They were deaf to his words and laying their garments at the feet of a young man called Saul they stoned Stephen to death. It is interesting to note that Stephen's vision tallied with what Jesus described to the high priests at his trial whereby they condemned him for

Part 4.

blasphemy, Matthew 26, vv63–68, which in turn was drawn from Psalm 110, verse 1 and Daniel 7, verse 13.

8. Saul consented to the action taken to stone Stephen not realising the impact it would have on his life. Further to Stephen's death a persecution took place against the church in Jerusalem scattering all save the apostles. Devout men buried Stephen, but this Saul ravaged the church arresting those who followed Jesus and casting them into prison, men and women. If that was not reaction enough imagine the surprise when Saul encountered Jesus for himself on the road to Damascus and how it changed him. However ministry and conversion continued meanwhile through Uncle Peter and John who went to Samaria when they heard they had received the word of God there but not the Holy Spirit so they baptized them and laid their hands on them to receive Holy Spirit. (John 4, vv1–42 recounts how Jesus took his disciples there and the woman at the well believed him and brought others.) One Simon wanted to buy the power of the Holy Spirit so he could lay on hands to impart it. Uncle Peter roundly rebuked him as he was not genuine in his belief if he thought he could buy it and profit from it. He repented and begged Uncle Peter's curse would not befall him. Further ministry took place through deacons like Philip so the Word reached Ethiopia through the eunuch in the queen's service, who raised many sons of the word in turn.

9. As Saul set out to Damascus to arrest its adherents and so suppress the Way as those who followed what the apostles taught were labelled, so Uncle Peter's ministry grew and took him further afield. Still affiliated to Judaism it was seen as a charismatic movement and deviant from regular orthodoxy, but it contained new seeds of truth as opposed to other communities that existed at the time, maybe building on the quote by Jesus that John recorded (14, verse 6) 'I am the way, and the truth, and the life'. Like all religions focusing on God as we know Him or their god in their own view there is common ground or a way of practice that mirror each other. Who knows what else Jesus experienced, studied or

discovered in the years before he began his ministry that developed how he understood what God and what the scriptures said to him, and how he would present that truth? Nevertheless the Holy Spirit gave Uncle Peter the impetus to preach the truth as revealed to him and as seen and heard by him.

He went down to Lydda and there healed Aeneas who had been bed ridden for eight years, and then in Joppa he raised Tabitha, also known as Dorcas (Gazelle), from the dead, a woman renowned for good works and sewing skills. He continued his stay there at the house of Simon the tanner.

10. From Caesarea by command of Cornelius, a centurion of the Italian Cohort, Uncle Peter received a summons following a vision by the former, a devout and philanthropic man himself. Before receiving the summons Uncle Peter was praying and fell in a trance centring on being hungry and offered a variety of foods with the directions to kill and eat. He refused on the grounds that the food was unclean whereupon he was reprimanded by God that what was clean for God was clean for men. It happened three times before the offering was drawn back into heaven. He was puzzling over the experience and what it meant when the men from Cornelius arrived and he realised it was God's intention to send him to the Gentiles. He was expected and when Cornelius worshipped him he denied that he was any more special than any other man, so what did he want? It was nothing more than to hear the Lord's good news. When the Holy Spirit fell on all who heard what he had to say about the Good News Uncle Peter's reaction was to confirm the work of the Holy Spirit amongst the Gentiles and baptize them.

11. When Uncle Peter returned to Jerusalem the orthodox followers of the Way, known as the Circumcision Party because they felt new converts should be treated as full Jewish members, were appalled that Gentiles had been converted. But when he explained the full story they gave God the glory that Gentiles, too, had been granted repentance unto life. Meanwhile following the martyrdom of Stephen many believers had dispersed but

Part 4.

continued to share the good news with fellow Jews. Some went to Antioch and preached to the Greeks who readily responded with belief. As a result the church in Jerusalem sent Barnabas to check it out and the numbers of believers grew considerably. He went to Tarsus to fetch Saul and they returned to Antioch to spend a year with the church there and it was here that all the disciples of the risen Lord were first called Christians.

When some prophets joined them from Jerusalem there was one, Agabus, who foretold a great famine that happened in the days of Claudius so the disciples resolved to collect relief for those believers in Judea and sent it to the Jerusalem elders in the safekeeping of Barnabas and Saul.

12. Herod set out to persecute the church and had James the brother of John beheaded and went on to arrest Uncle Peter, because it pleased the Jews, during the feast of Unleavened Bread. He was kept in prison under guard of four squads of soldiers with the intention of bringing him out to the people at the Passover. Despite being chained to soldiers and guarded behind locked doors he was woken up the night before his proposed public trial, commanded to dress and follow this vision. Amazed, he found himself out in the street, a free man. It could only be explained as an act of God, so he made his way to the house of Mary my mother. When he knocked on the door Rhoda the maid recognised his voice but in her joy to tell everyone rushed off without letting him in. Of course they disbelieved her despite the fact they had been praying for him! However since he persisted knocking they had to investigate and he had to tell them to keep quiet, before moving elsewhere.

In the aftermath there was great consternation with the soldiers and Herod, who having asked for evidence of the escape had the sentries executed and went down to Tyre and Sidon where he came to a bad end for not giving God the glory.

15. Inevitably the church fractured into parties maintaining tradition, Judaism as they knew it, and progressives moving with the Holy Spirit and a more modern outlook, which in turn was

exacerbated by the inclusion of Gentiles without imposing the burden of being Jewish upon them. Drawing on his recent experience at Caesarea Uncle Peter let common sense prevail so that the church in Jerusalem accepted that the Holy Spirit was received by Greeks in Antioch regardless of having to become recognized Jews as well. This suited all parties and the church sent Saul (now known as Paul after preaching the Word in Cyprus at Paphos) and Barnabas, along with Silas and Judas or Justus (Barsabbas) back to Antioch to confirm their becoming disciples, or rather Christians being the derivative in Greek for followers of Christ as they came to be called. When the latter two returned to Jerusalem Paul and Barnabas remained in Antioch.

Soon after Paul proposed a return journey through the cities where they had preached and set up the roots of a local church. I had been with them having been a first hand witness of many things during our Lord's earthly life and Barnabas wanted me to go with them. Paul refused as sometime back in Pamphylia I had withdrawn from working with them to do my own thing. As a result Paul and Barnabas disagreed and I sailed with Barnabas to Cyprus. This virtually ended my contact with Paul energetically setting up church groups and he was joined by Luke the doctor shortly after before setting sail for Macedonia from Troy with Silas as his close companion, so the first hand record of the early church fell to Luke to relate as an ongoing eye witness in Paul's company.

Paul went on to suffer much for the gospel and always paid his own way working as a tent maker. He did persuade Timothy to take me with him to Rome as Paul began to realise the day of the Lord's return was not immediate and the gospel should be recorded for future generations and for the benefit of the church to know her own story since I was a living eye witness of many things. Luke, too, researched the background for a version of the Gospel as he heard it passed down from others he encountered and no doubt interviewed. He then offered a gospel that preceded what he recorded and witnessed in the Acts of the Apostles for the benefit of anyone wanting to know the story behind the faith they

Part 4.

were prepared to accept. It is a valid second hand record of Uncle Peter's journey to spiritual maturity.

Postscript

Thoughts Round Peter

THE EPISTLES OF PETER

DID PETER WRITE THE two epistles attributed to him as the author? It is likely the first letter could have been, bearing in mind that it was considered Peter was martyred at 65 AD—hence the reference at the end of John's gospel to being taken where he did not want to go and his arms stretched out. Its content pre-empts the persecution of the Church in Asia Minor and he may have visited in the later 40s the church in Galatia which is mentioned by Paul in his letter to the Galatians (2, vv11–22) covering Paul criticizing Peter for inconsistency over eating with Gentiles. Peter did not preach that Gentiles could be saved by circumcision and the law but in Paul's eyes he betrayed the freedom of the Gospel and the gift of Grace by reverting back to Jewish law and custom despite being the first to open the Gospel to the Gentiles. One step forward and two steps back. There is no doubt that there was pressure from the Jews in Jerusalem who followed the Way to conform to the Jewish traditions which is exactly what Jesus wanted to free people from! Part of the argument would rest on whether remaining Jewish would give Christians the cover of religious toleration allowed to Jews until the fall of Jerusalem in 70 AD, when the Romans defeated a Jewish rebellion and dispersed them, against a freedom of expression as Christians in the mould Christ left for people.

Peter as the prominent elder of the early church had the authority of experience and as eye witness to encourage the overseas church in Asia Minor to live by example to win acceptance by other Gentiles and he dwells on the image of Christ as the rejected stone becoming the corner stone of this new understanding and practice of faith quoting from Isaiah 8,v14; 28, v16, and Psalm 118, v22, and quoted by Jesus in Matthew 21, v42.

In his conclusion from Babylon (think Rome as bad) he includes greetings from his son Mark. Son or nephew? Mark or John Mark? Would Mary in Acts 12, verse 12 be his wife and make it a good reason for obviously not staying if there was to be a search for him after his miraculous escape so Mark therefore would be his son? How much of Mark is there in John's Gospel? These are questions we can only guess at and piece together if they coincide. Suffice to say in the New Testament some players have alternative names and others similar names so reading has to be measured to get the best grasp.

The second letter of Peter is much later, maybe 150 AD, and a different style. It claims authenticity by citing he was a witness of the transfiguration, so there was a story in circulation about Jesus and the inner three disciples. It is a reminder of the truth of the gospel and that the delay in the expected Parousia, or second coming of Christ, is that God delays giving time for all men to repent which is his wish. Obviously by attributing either or both letters to Peter it gave them greater weight and authority when there was important news, guidance or correction to convey.

RESURRECTION

Our evidence for the resurrection of Jesus does not rest on Peter alone. The other disciple was there and Mary Magdalen was commissioned to tell the others having seen Jesus—the criteria to be an apostle was to have seen and be sent by Jesus, and she became the first—and the gospels tell us of appearances to many others in what must have been a very active time of the Holy Spirit. It

POSTSCRIPT

is an ongoing speculation that Mark as a boy spying out on Jesus saw much and may have been tasked by Jesus to help in various ways. Was he the young man in white in the tomb Mark 16, verse 5, but the women were so flabbergasted they did not recognise him? Maybe one of a few cameo parts in his story?

While the resurrection is hard to believe since it breaks the laws of nature that hold human mortality in check and balance, albeit that it is balanced by the extraordinary stories of his incarnation and birth in Matthew and Luke, there is something about the ordered empty tomb and the fulfilment of Jesus' predictions in the Gospels that point towards those mentioned in the story as eye witnesses being genuine, despite disbelieving the women in the first place as it was beyond belief! They saw and recognised the risen Lord Jesus and the story continues to unfold to this day. The breaking of bread is a familiar everyday memorial for a gathered community to feed on his body and so embody him.

Delving deeper while Matthew and Luke relate Jesus' physical birth Mark and John start with his spiritual birth at baptism. Matthew and Luke anticipate or include ascension as an end of his earthly life while Mark leaves the story in limbo for us to fathom the truth that others there find hard to believe and John finishes with the restoration of Peter and the mystery surrounding the last man standing, again perhaps pointing to ourselves!

ETERNAL LIFE

There are a number of references in the Gospels to Jesus mentioning and explaining Eternal (or Age Lasting) Life. Not just for the here and now but futuristic reaching into a life beyond or life continuing in a new dimension after death. On another level it can be seen as a level of belief that will not die out. The synoptic gospels all have a couple of references in passing but John, trying to get into the gospel rather than just relaying the story, has 9 references and a further 6 in his first epistle. Paul also quotes eternal life in his letters as does the writer of the Epistle to the Hebrews.

John 3,v15; 4,v36; 5,v39; 6,vv 54, 68; 10,v28; 12,v25; 17,v2–3.

1 John 1,v2; 2,v25;3,v15; 5,vv 11,13, 20.

Of these John 5,v39 stands out where Jesus criticizes his detractors for searching the scriptures for eternal life that actually point to him but they will not accept the truth before their very eyes nor the attestation by God.

In John 6, vv54 and 68 Jesus teaches to his disciples that his words are spirit and life and it is Peter who responds that you have the words of Eternal Life.

In 1John 5, a general letter in itself of encouragement to gathered believers at large from an acclaimed eye witness, the writer is at pains, verse 11, to endorse that Eternal Life is a gift of God and this is a testimony of faith that the Son of God is life. Come verse 13 the letter is to endorse that belief in the Son is to know you have Eternal Life. Lastly verse 20 acknowledging the true God and Eternal Life are combined with the person being in Jesus Christ the Son of God. Reading John's gospel and his focus on the symbolism of bread and wine remind us that through communion and the breaking of bread together we embody Christ.

Taking a broader look at Peter, despite in John 6, verse 68, admitting Jesus has the words of eternal life, his preaching and outlining the gospel focus more on belief in Jesus for forgiveness and salvation. Belief in Jesus is sufficient in itself. The impetuous fisherman at once recognizing Jesus as the Christ (Matthew 16, v16; Mark 8, v29; Luke 9, v20) the next moment cannot understand the weakness of the Christ who has been built up in the common mind to bring new and powerful rule to mankind. What he learns about the Christ at the Transfiguration as recorded in the synoptic gospels he finds it hard to apply, though given he is charged at the time to tell no one. On the other hand in John's gospel, 1,v 41, it is Andrew, to whom Jesus is pointed out by John the Baptist as the Lamb of God, who goes to find his brother Peter saying 'We have found the Messiah (Christ)', and it is Martha before Lazarus' tomb, his raising back to life, and his restoration to his sisters, who confesses to Jesus, 11, v27, 'Yes, Lord; I believe that you are the Christ, the Son of God, he who is coming into the world.' Ironically Peter finds that strength is found in weakness, the answer

Postscript

in silence. It is not what one would expect until belief ushers in a different experience and outlook, frustratingly not at first securing much sought after peace in many fields of confrontation. Again the mini apocalypse in Mark 13, v1–17 warns of wars and rumours of war and other tribulation before the coming of the Son of Man.

The weakness of Peter as a man is replaced, when an eye witness to the risen Lord and after his redemption by the risen Jesus following the catch of a draft of fish John 21, with an inner strength and conviction so that the Holy Spirit within gives new power. Indeed the fisherman becomes not only a fisher of men, Matthew 4, v19 and Mark 1, V17, but also a tower of the early church and a healing figure in the ilk of the earthly Jesus. It was a turnaround.

This begs the question what does the life of Peter have to tell us about eternal life? His faith became solid as a rock, and he shared his belief not only in Jesus but as a witness of the resurrection. Jesus was Eternal Life to him. It was costly and Peter died for it, but within what he believed of Jesus as the Christ there was a foundation of hope that Eternal Life in this life was a beginning and not a blank end. The end may be painful too. Yes mortal life would end, dust would return to dust, ashes to ashes, and earth to earth, but it would not crush the spirit from the soul in the soul's search for a return to God leaving behind the materialistic and the temporal and joining the Creator in the new dimension of His Spirit and timelessness. Indeed Jesus was the door to a new sheepfold 'I am the door of the sheep', John 10, verse 7, and verse 9 'I am the door and if anyone enters by me he will be saved'. Eternal Life accepted in this life leads to a new life in God's sheepfold.

Eternal Life is the thread that leads to the Kingdom of God and to Heaven where those who accept salvation through belief in Christ follow his Way and are fast tracked avoiding the Accuser and the Day of Judgement. The latter featured as very much part of Jewish thought at the time and is behind later medieval Christian understanding leading to hell and purgatory (Dante's Divine Comedy gives a good view.) It must be understood, therefore, that on the Day of Judgement the soul stood accused and was weighed against a feather for likely sin (falling short.) The accuser was

Satan, and in order to have evidence to present in the heavenly law court he was also the tempter. (The Lord's prayer in Matthew 6, v13 can also read 'Do not bring us to the time of trial but deliver us from the evil one.') The classic example is Jesus' temptations in the wilderness where scripture is used against Jesus by Satan and answered with scripture underlining obedience to God. Hence in the bidding to confession in Anglican liturgy there is a reference to our having an advocate (defending counsel 1 John 2, v1) giving us true hope and also references to eternal life there and in the absolution. However belief in and acceptance of Jesus is sufficient in itself to keep us on that thread of eternal life weaved through mankind for all time. If we fall short we can confess our failure, find forgiveness, and be restored. As Jesus is recorded saying in the Gospels he has defeated Satan 'I saw Satan fall like lightening' Luke 10, verse 18, and John 16, verse 11 'the ruler of this world is judged', and John 12, verse 31, 'now shall the ruler of this world be cast out' for instance. It follows that eternal life on another level is life without Satan (Job 1), without temptation, where belief in Jesus, love of God, and love of neighbour lead the way for mankind.

If this thread leads to heaven what is that? It can be none other than God's presence where time past and time future are absorbed into time present and all become timeless. Considering we are made by God for his own pleasure and companionship our selfishness causes us to fall short (sin) and we may be cut off. The opposite of Eternal Life being Gehenna (Matt. 5, vv22 & 29), the municipal rubbish dump outside Jerusalem in the Hinnom valley that burned 24/7—hence hell and Hades (in Greek or Sheol in Hebrew.) It was also identified with Topheth in the Old Testament where the idol of Molech was set up and infants were sacrificed until Josiah's reign. While God would have all restored we can waste our lives, but what is of God, that is spirit, returns to God for God is spirit as Jesus tells us (John 4, v24). Without God, son and Holy Spirit we are but dust and ashes.

If it seems selfish of God to create the world and us for his own pleasure, as recited in the first chapters of Genesis and the Garden of Eden, there is the opposite when that love causes Him

POSTSCRIPT

to give Himself in his Son to redeem us on the cross, which in turn ties in with Jesus endorsing the commandment 'love your neighbour as yourself.' Not only does He therefore love us as he loves Himself in His creation but we in turn are encouraged to be outward looking to serve others, the other example being the Maundy Thursday foot washing, John 13, vv1–20. God leads the way in the Son and the Spirit is there to help us.

Here the prayer of Jesus to be glorified (John 17, vv1–5) rings true: power from God 'to give eternal life to all thou hast given him (thy Son). And this is eternal life, that they know thee the only true God, and Jesu Christ whom thou hast sent. I glorified thee on earth. . . .'

The challenge to all is to follow where Jesus led and find Eternal Life for ourselves.

I WOULD SUM UP PETER AS FOLLOWS IN A SONNET:

> John pointed Jesus to Andrew, and another,
> Who followed to where he was staying
> And spent the day exploring, praying.
> Observant, he found his brother
> To share revelations so fabulous.
> Peter, quick to react, impetuous,
> Left his nets to be a spiritual landmark
> Though to begin with his faith was stark:
> The shoal of fish—incredulous;
> A suffering Messiah—scandalous;
> His pre-conceptions—idolatrous?
> Guilty of denial—disastrous.
> He became a Samson for the Church
> As Andrew enabled folk in their search.

(Included in my volume of verse *Cameos of Faith*, published Wipf and Stock, 2022.)

Index

The Old Testament references in Mark's gospel

An aid to understanding something of the background to Jesus' life and ministry and how Mark moulded his story round the narrative of scripture to throw new light on it.

1v3: Voice in the wilderness—Isaiah 40,v3.

1v11: Beloved sn—Psalm 2,v7; Is 40,v1.

1v44: Showing the priest your cure Leviticus 13,v49; 14, vv2-33.

2v23: Breaking the sabbath—Deuteronomy 23,v29.

2v26: Eating the shew bread—1 Samuel 21, vv1-6; 2 Sam 8,v17.

2v27: On the sabbath—Exodus 23,v12; Deut 5,v14.

3v27: Raiding the strong man's house—Is 49, vv24-25.

4v12: Remaining blind, missing the point—Is 6,v9.

5v25: Woman with hemorhagge—Lev 25,v25.

6v18: Herod's adultery—Lev 18,v16, 20,v21.

7v10: 5th Commandment—Ex 20,v12; Deut 5,v6; Lev 20,v9.

7v35: Deaf & dumb healed -Is 35, vv5-6.

8v17: No bread, lack of understanding—Is 6, vv9-10.

9v38: Others working in Jesus' name—Numbers 11, vv27-29.

9v49: Saltiness of salt—Lev 2,v13. Entry to the Kingdom is for the pure in heart—thus salt preserves, fire purifies symbolizing consecration.

10v4: Divorce—Deut 24, vv1–4.

10v6: Man created—Genesis 1,v27, 5,v2.

10v7: Marriage—Gen 2,v24

10v19: 10 commandments—Deut 5, vv16–20.

10v23: Difficult for rich to enter the Kingdom of God—Ps 52,v7, 62,v10.

11v9: Hosanna—Ps 118,v26.

11v17: Cleansing the temple—Is 56,v7; Jeremiah 7,v11.

12v1: Parable of the Vineyard—Is 5, vv1–7.

12v10: Rejected foundation stone—Ps 118, vv22–23.

12v19: Mosaic law re widow of childless man—Deut 25,v5.

12v26: God of the living—Ex 3,v6.

12v29: The great commandment—Deut 6,v4.

12v31: Love neighbour—Lev 19,v18.

12v32: The one God—Deut 4,v39; Is 45,v6&14, 46,v9.

12v33: Love God truly—I Sam 15,v22; Hosea 6,v6; Micah 6, vv6–8.

12v36: David on David?—Ps 110,v1.

12v41: Paying temple tribute—2 Kings 12,v9.

13v12: Brother betrays brother—Mic 7,v6.

13v14: Desolating sacrilege—Daniel 9,v27; 11,v31; 12,v14.

13v19: Tribulation—Dan 9,v26; 12,v1; Joel 2,v2.

13v24: Days to come—Zephaniah 1,v15.

13v26; Son of Man coming in the clouds—Dan 7,v13.

14v7: supporting the poor—Deut 15,v11.

14v12: Feast of Unleavened Bread—Ex 12,v11.

Index

14v24: Blood of the covenant—Ex 24,v8.

14v27: Shepherd struck—Zechariah 13,v7.

14v50: Forsaking friends—Ps 88,v8.

14v61: Silent before accuser—Is 53,v7.

14v63: Garments rent as a sign—Numbers 14,v6.

14v64: Blasphemy—Lev 12,v16.

15v5; Silence of Jesus—Is 53,v7

15v24: Jesus' clothes divided by lot—Ps22,v18.

15v29: Jesus' own words used in accusation—Ps22,v7.

15v31: Jesus taunted—Ps 22,v8.

15v34: Jesus cries out—Ps 22,v1.

15v36: Vinegar to drink—Ps 69,v21.

15v40: Those looking on—Ps 38, v11.

15v62: Day of Preparation—Deut 21, vv22-23.

16 v8: End of earliest original text as known.

16 vv9-20: A postscript of what followed added with hindsight—maybe years later as style and words very different.

NB: How much the Old Testament dictated the life and ministry of Jesus besides being the backbone that moulded how Mark thought, wrote and set a style for someone whose first language was not Greek in which all the New Testament was first written.

The Fishermen's Boat

MARK TELLS US PETER used a casting net, as hinted by John when Andrew went to find him having spent time with Jesus after John the Baptist had pointed him out. Luke has Peter owning a boat and fishing with James and John sons of Zebedee who also owned boats.

In fact a boat from those times was discovered on the shore of Lake Tiberius/Sea of Galilee in 1986 which took some 12 years to preserve with wax. It measured 27 ft X 7.5 ft with a draft of 7.3ft. Certainly big enough to ride out a storm with Jesus asleep in the stern. It was flat bottomed to work close inshore, made of cedar planks fastened to ribs, with four staggered places for rowers and a mast.

It was obviously a thriving business to supply Jerusalem and in the 1970s a drawing of a fishing boat on a dressed stone was discovered by the English archaeologist from the British School of Archaeology in Jerusalem, Archie Walls, in the old quarry covered by the crypt of the church of the Holy Sepulchre generally considered the site of the tomb where they laid Jesus. It is also considered that the drawing served as a sign for the site of the fish shop selling fish from Galilee.

Afterword

Toddy Hoare's imaginative re-telling of the Apostle Peter's story gives us an accessible and insightful account of the life and work of the early church. What shines through Hoare's approach to Saint Peter's ministry is just how precarious it was. . .not just living hand-to-mouth, but also figuring out where the next call to be comes from and where it leads next. This is an intriguing and unusual book which will resonate with all who engage with it.

PROFESSOR MARTYN PERCY is Provost Theologian, Ming Hua College, Hong Kong; Professor of Religion and Culture, University of Saint Joseph, Macao; Research Prof., Institut für Christkatholische, Theologische Fakultät, Universität Berne, CH; Canon Theologian, Convocation of Episcopal Churches, Europe; Senior Research Associate, James Hutton Institute, Aberdeen, Scotland UK.

www.ingramcontent.com/pod-product-compliance
Lightning Source LLC
Chambersburg PA
CBHW071748040426
42446CB00012B/2496